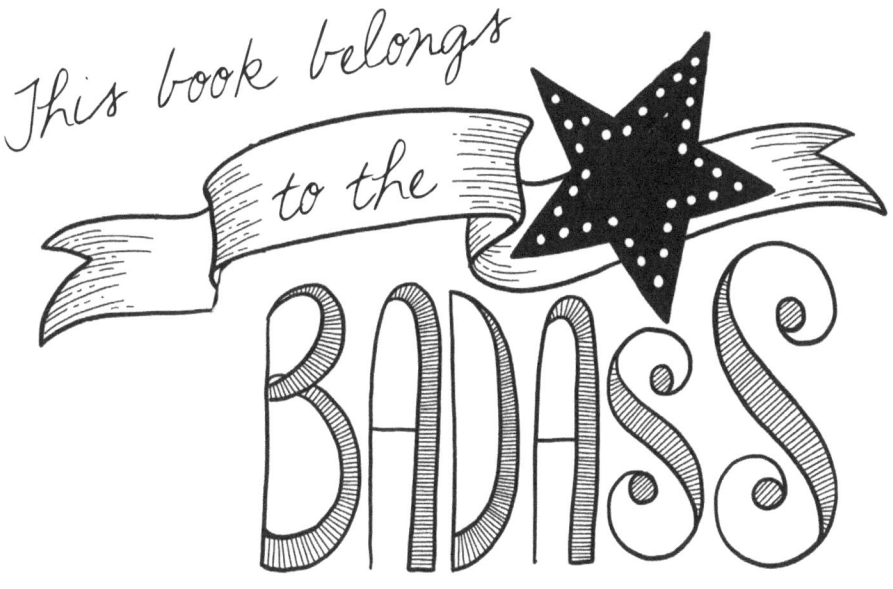

This book belongs to the **BADASS**

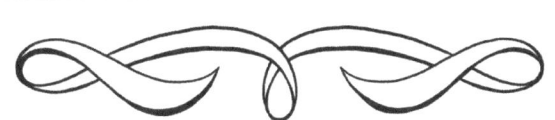

This book is published by Creative Collective Design
Copyright © 2017 by Creative Collective Design

All rights reserved. Published and distributed
in the United States by Creative Collective Design

www.creativecollectivedesign.com

ISBN 978-0-9994392-0-3

Manufactured in the United States

First Edition

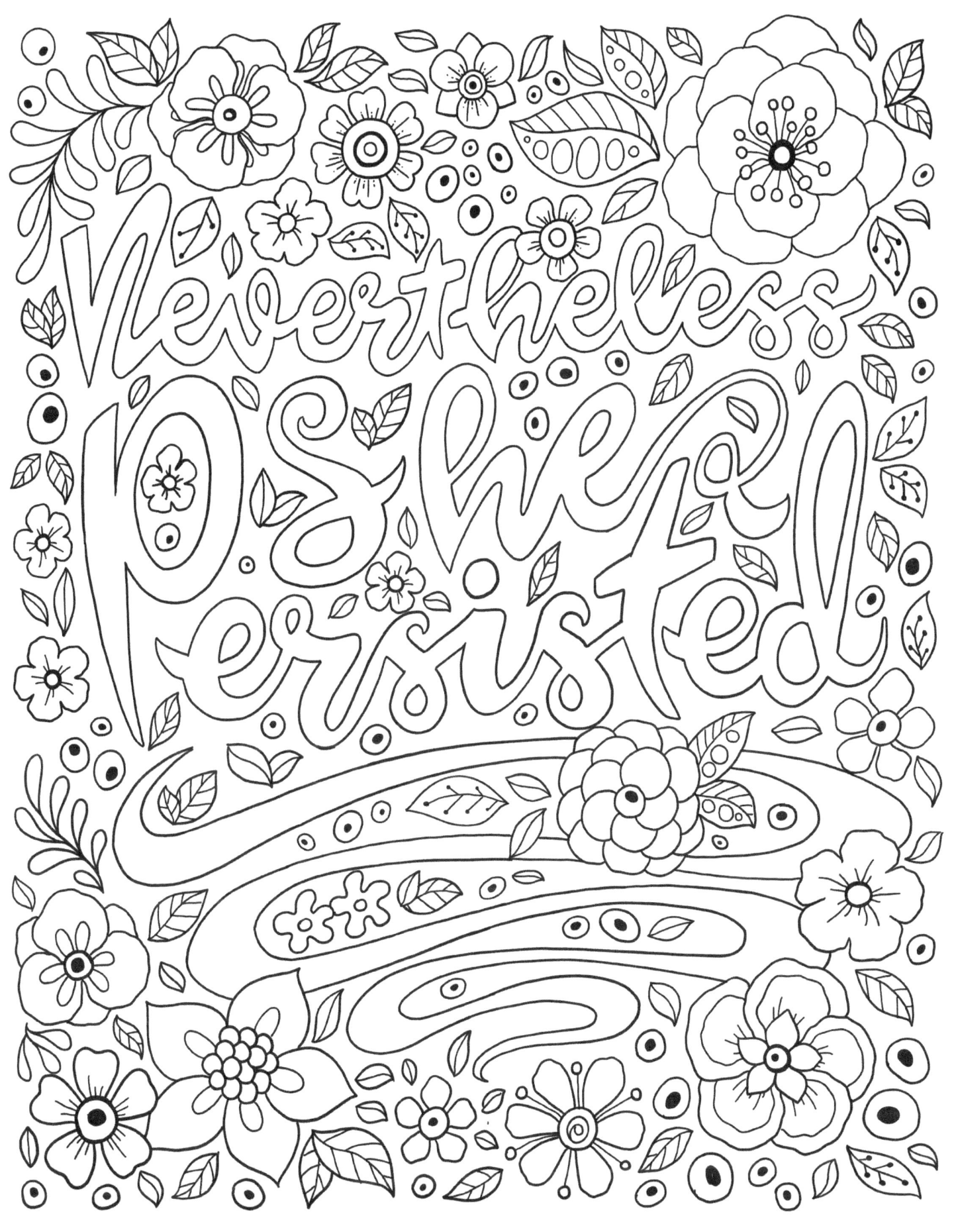

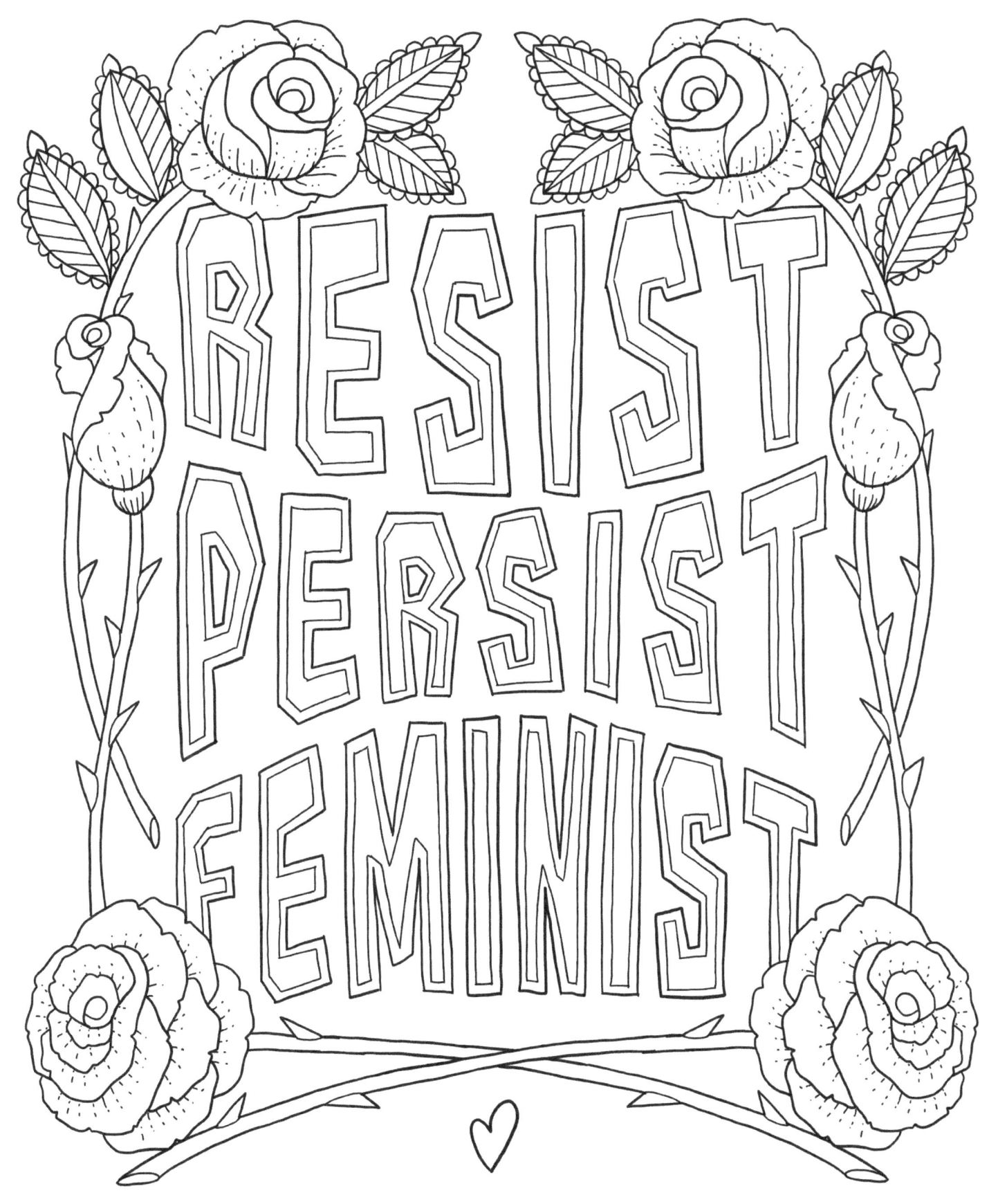

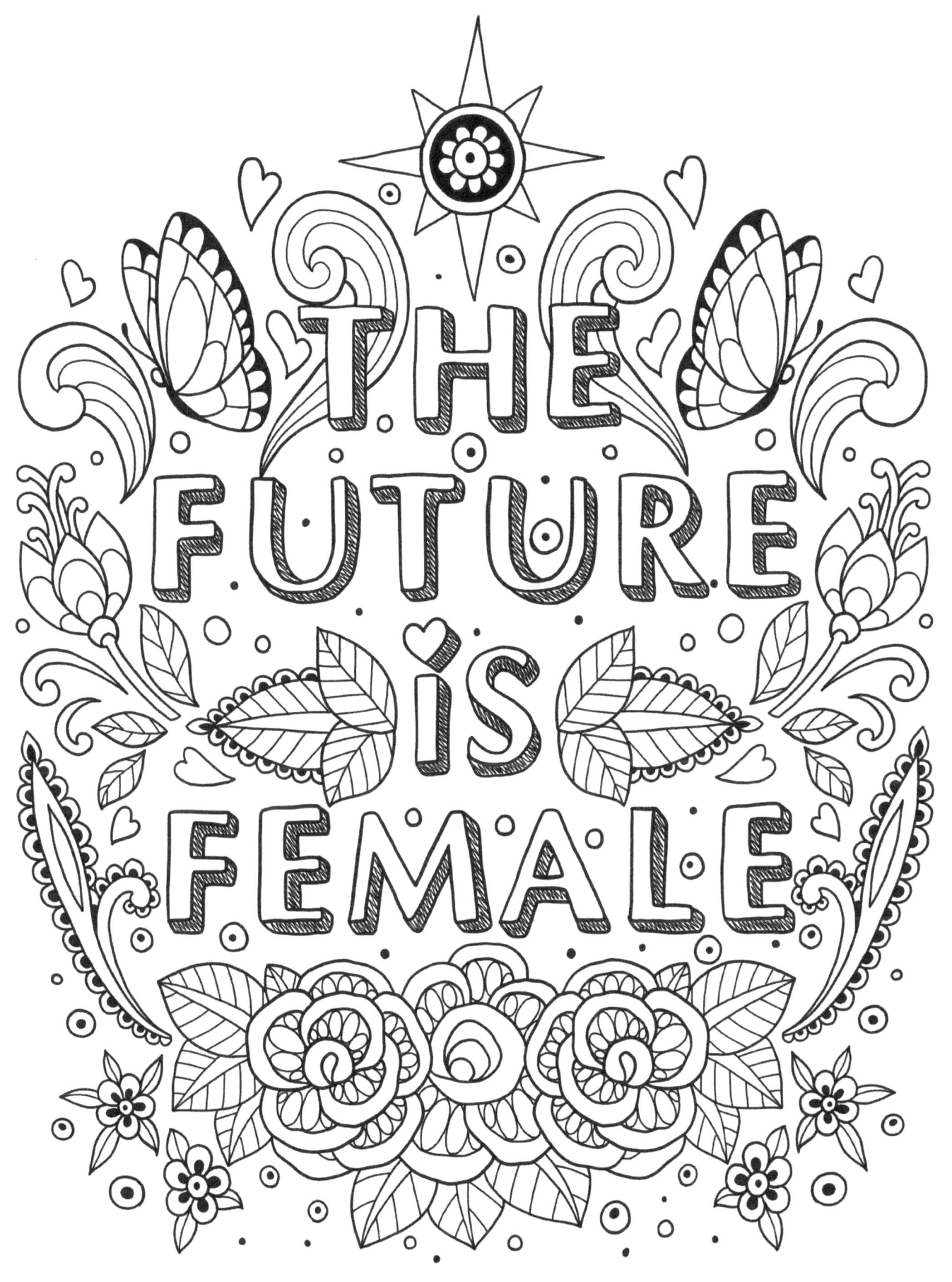

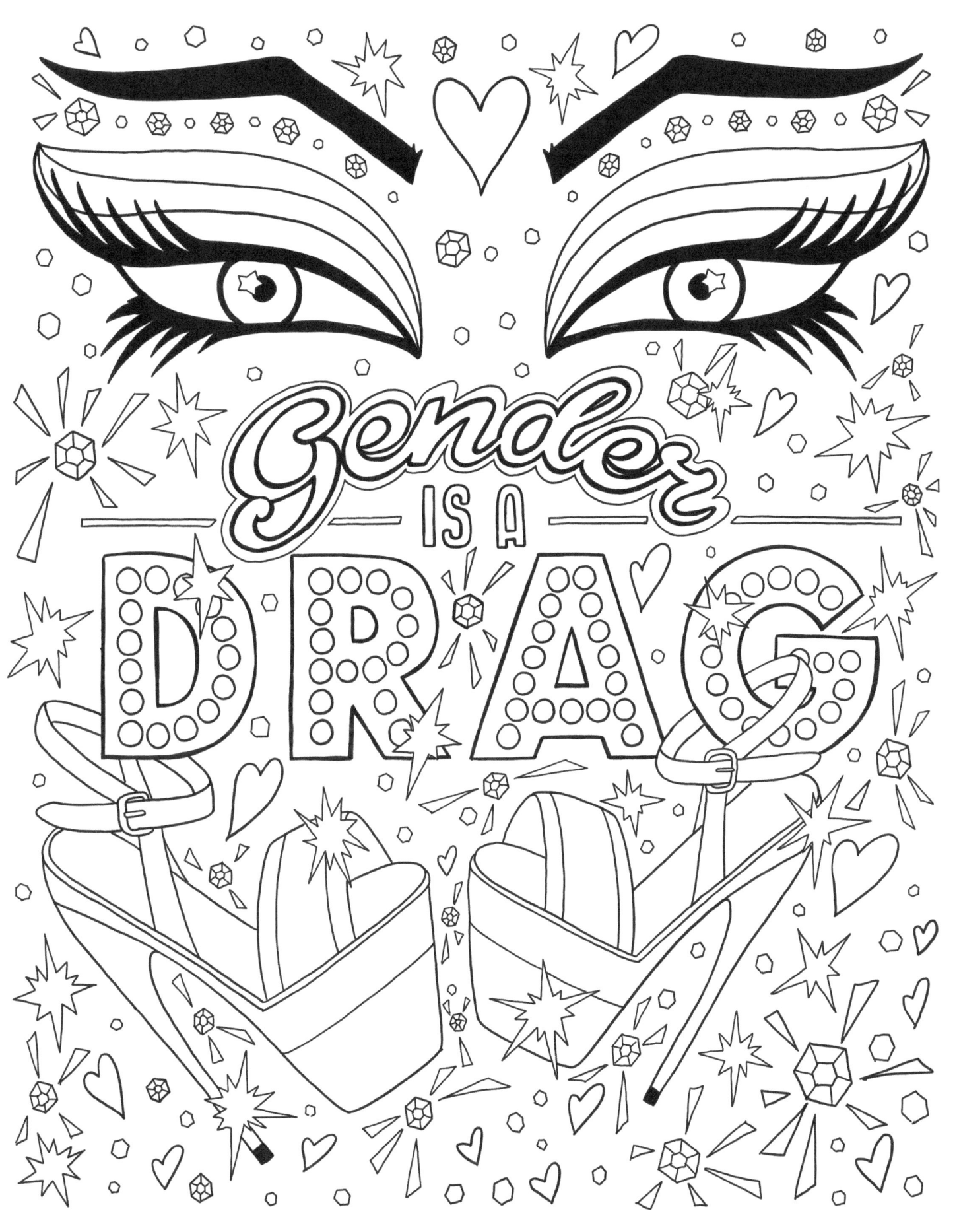

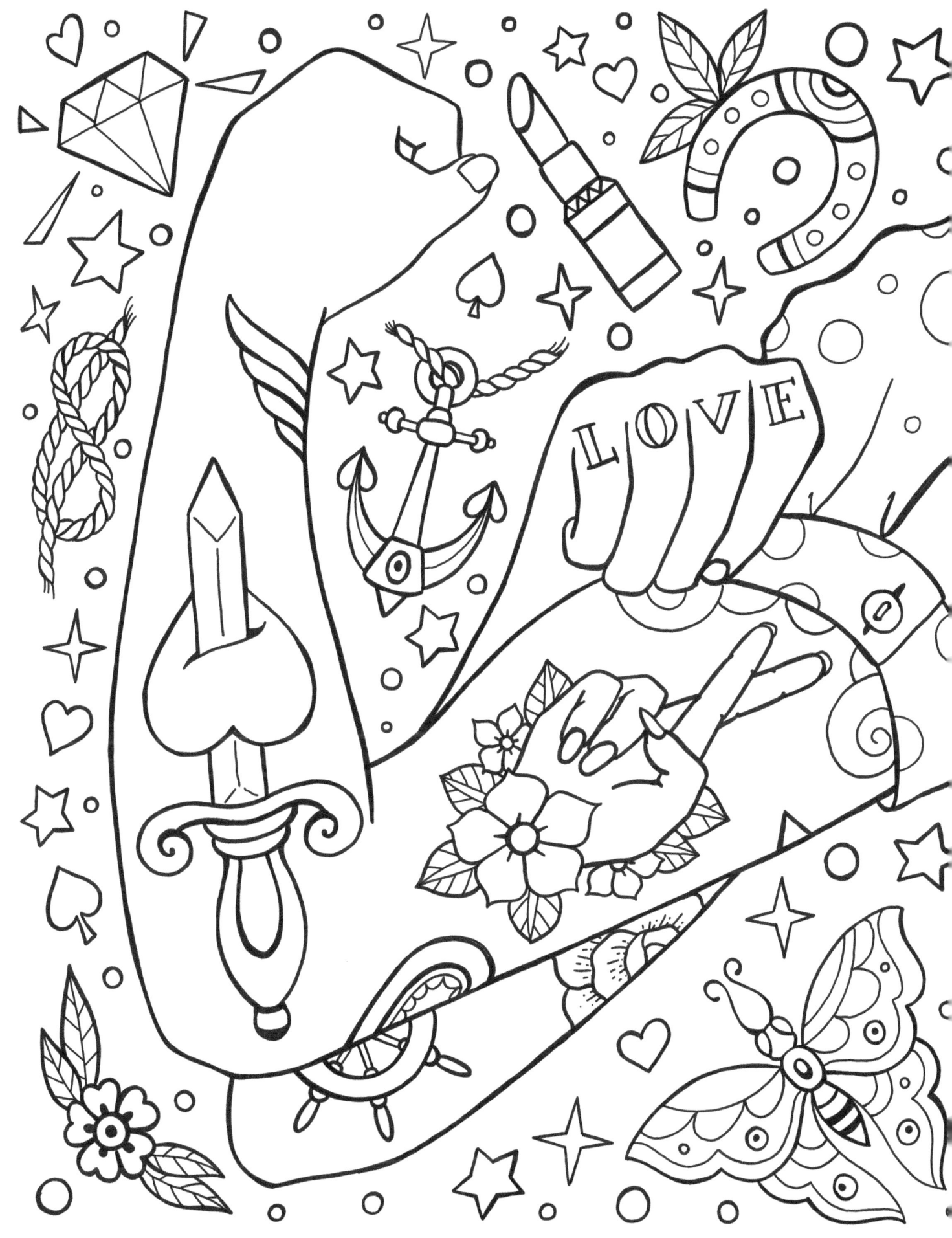

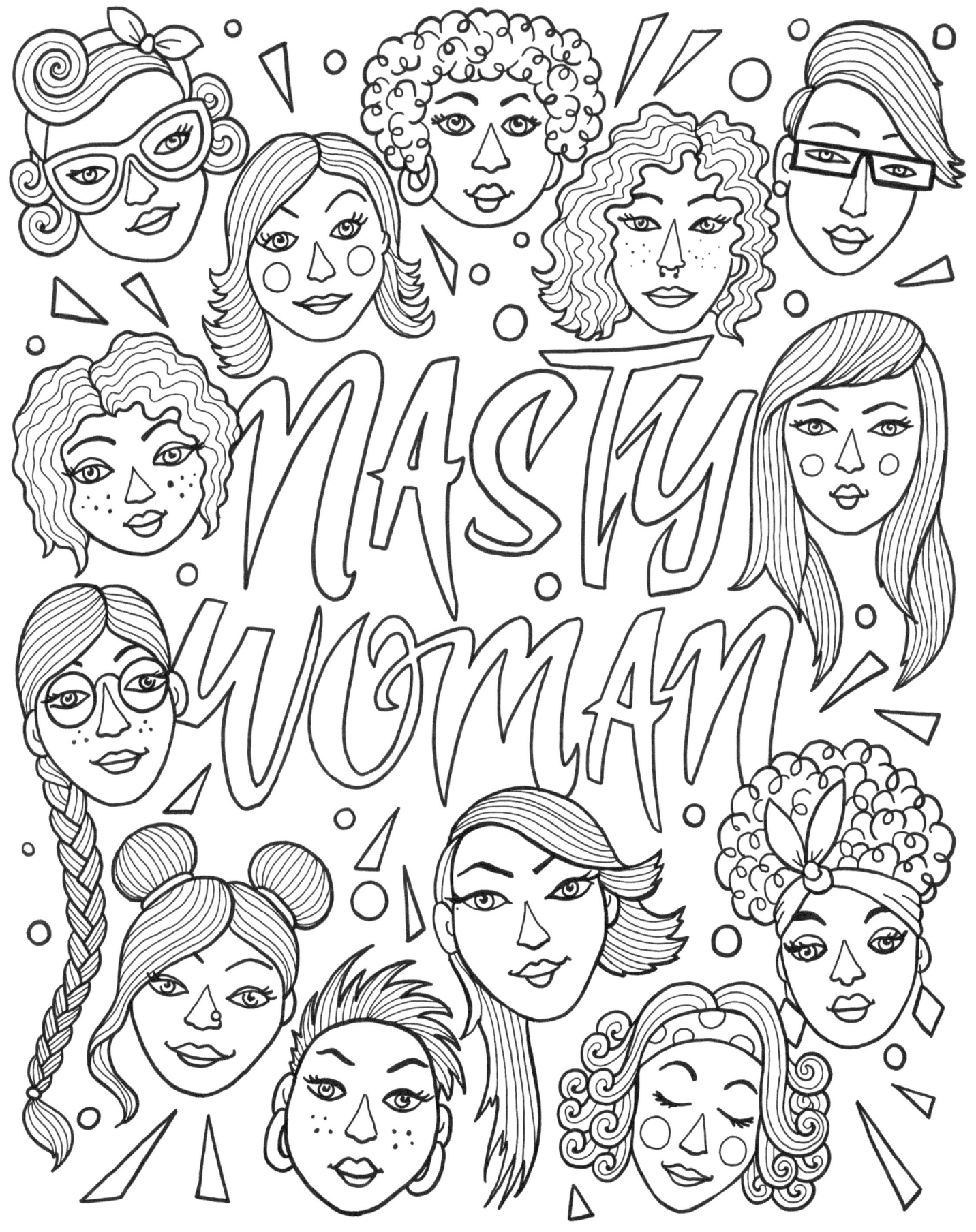

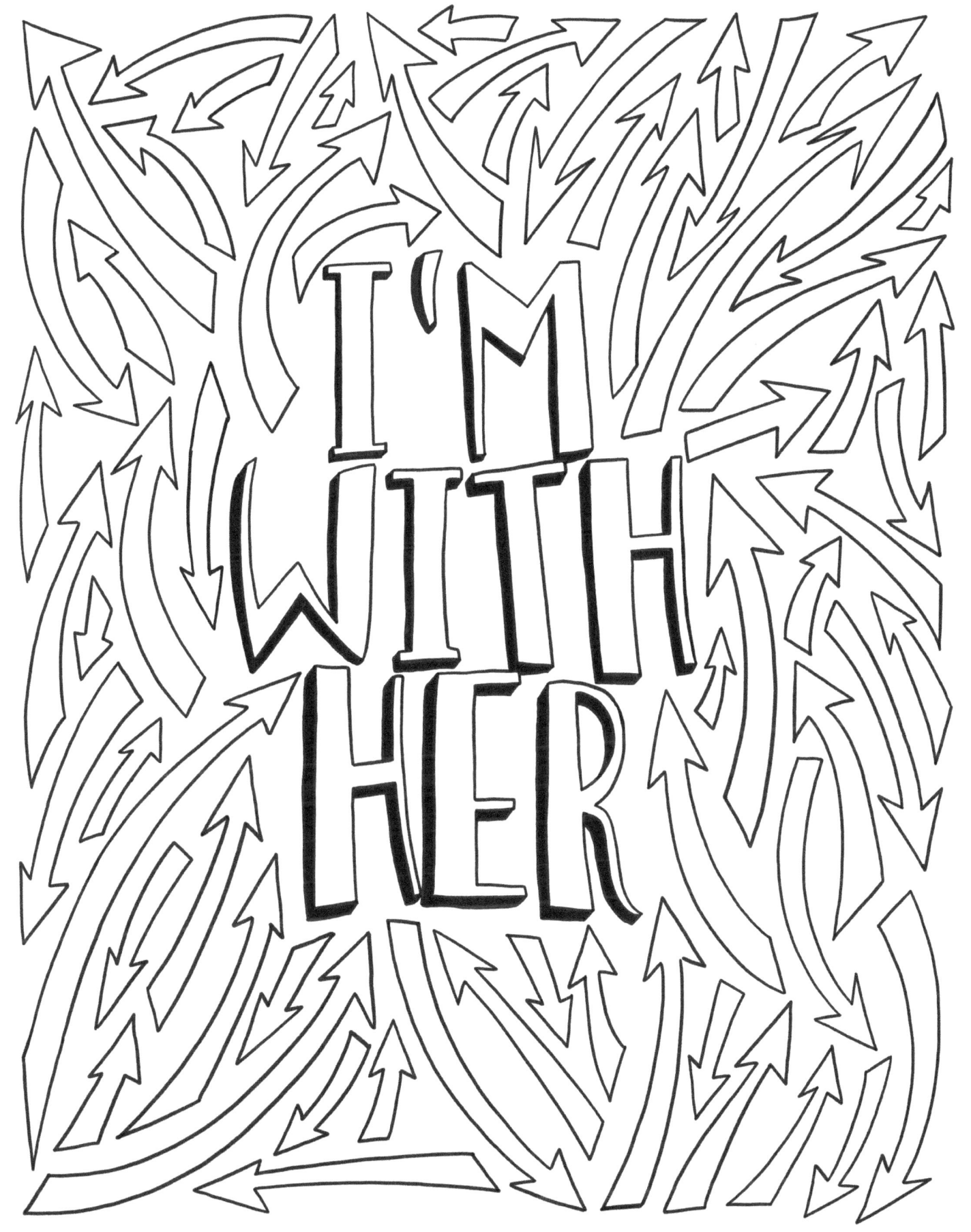

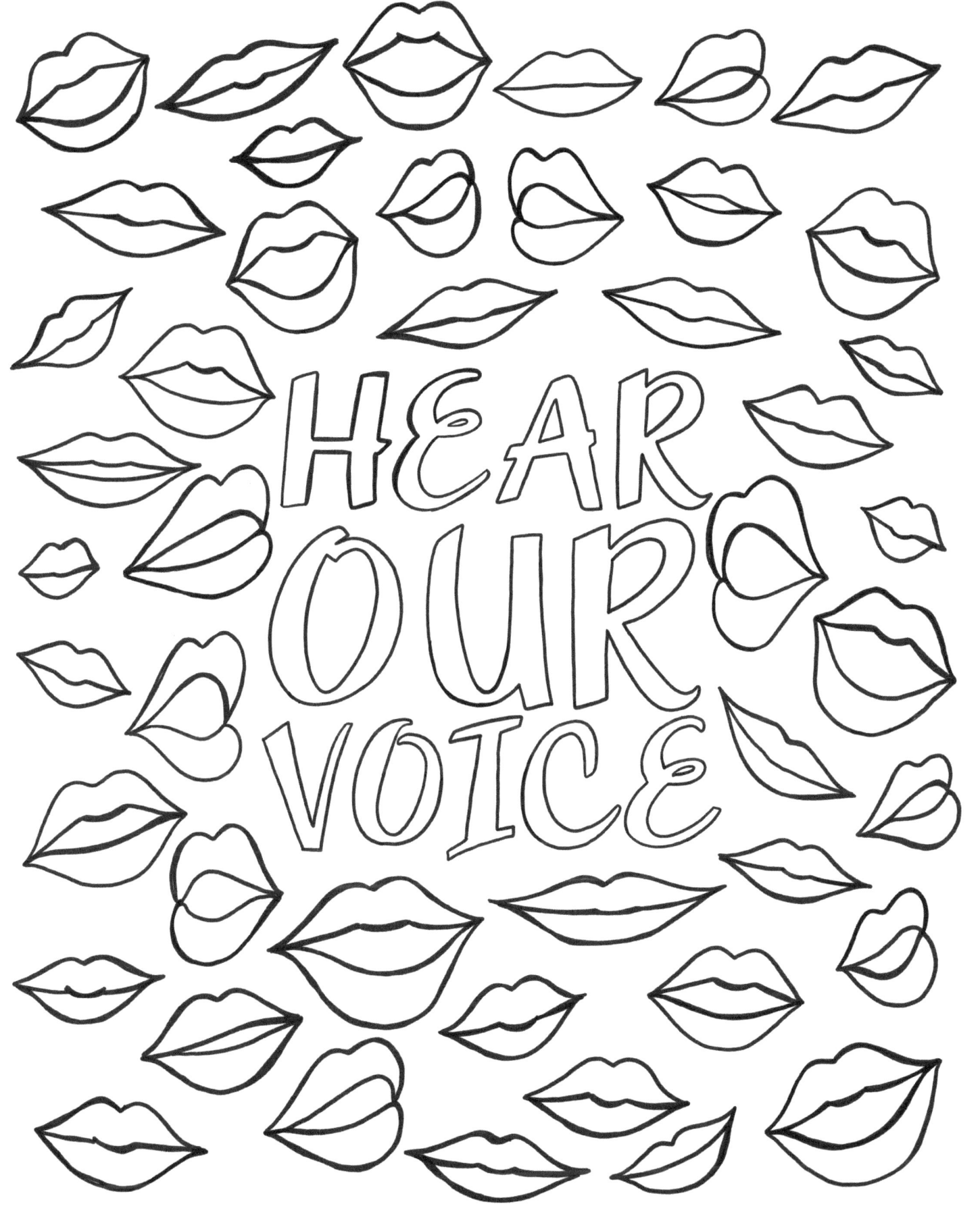

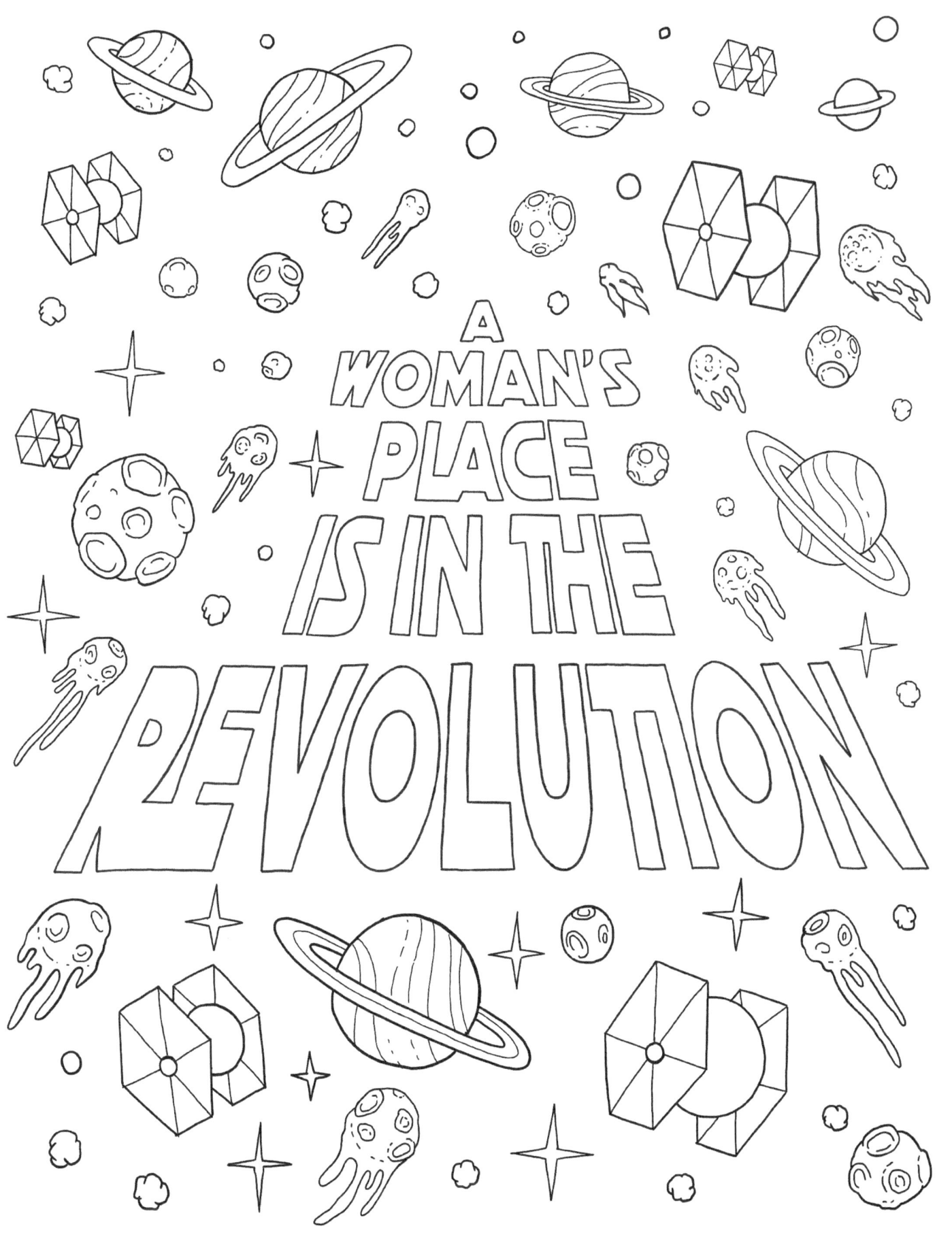

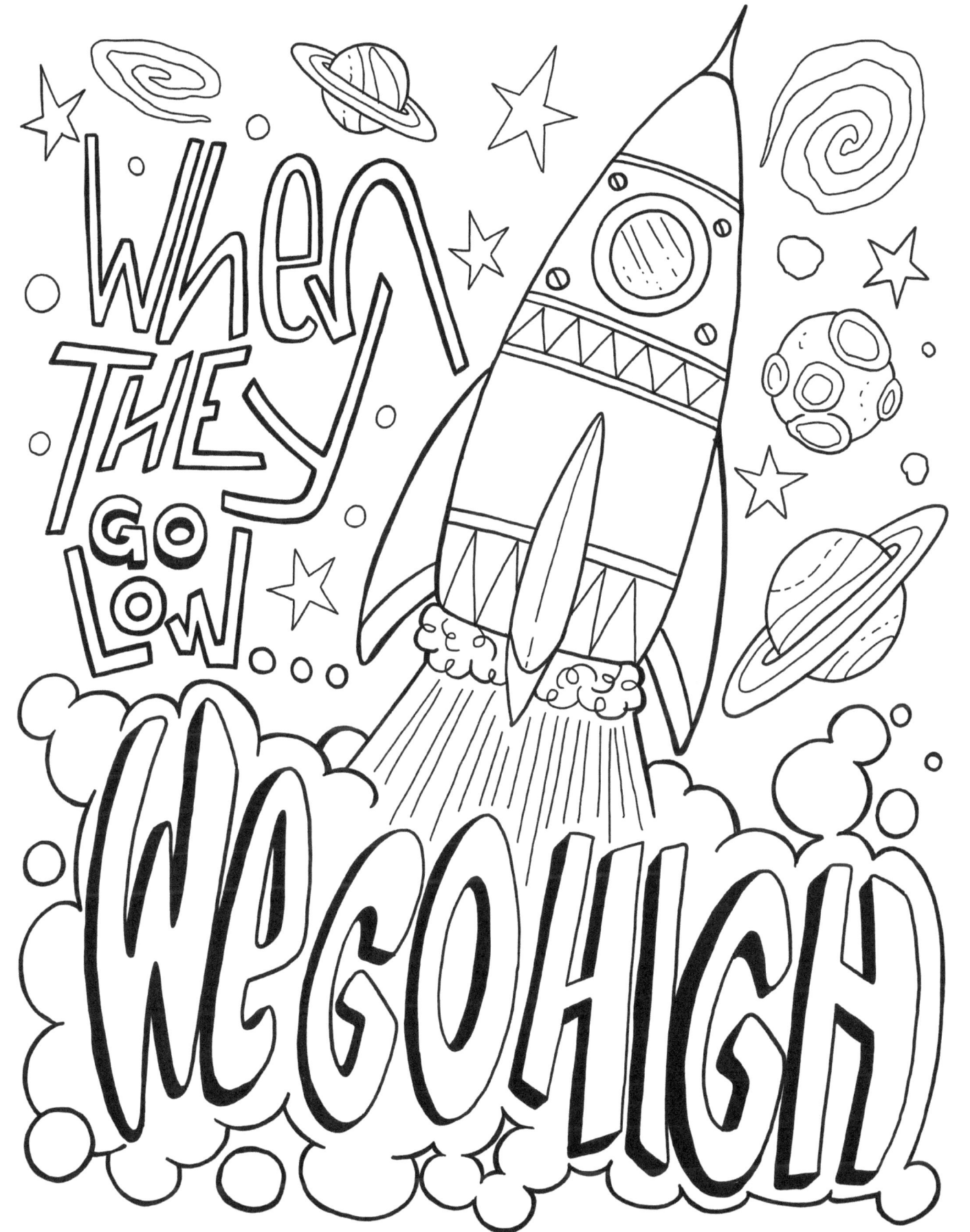

6

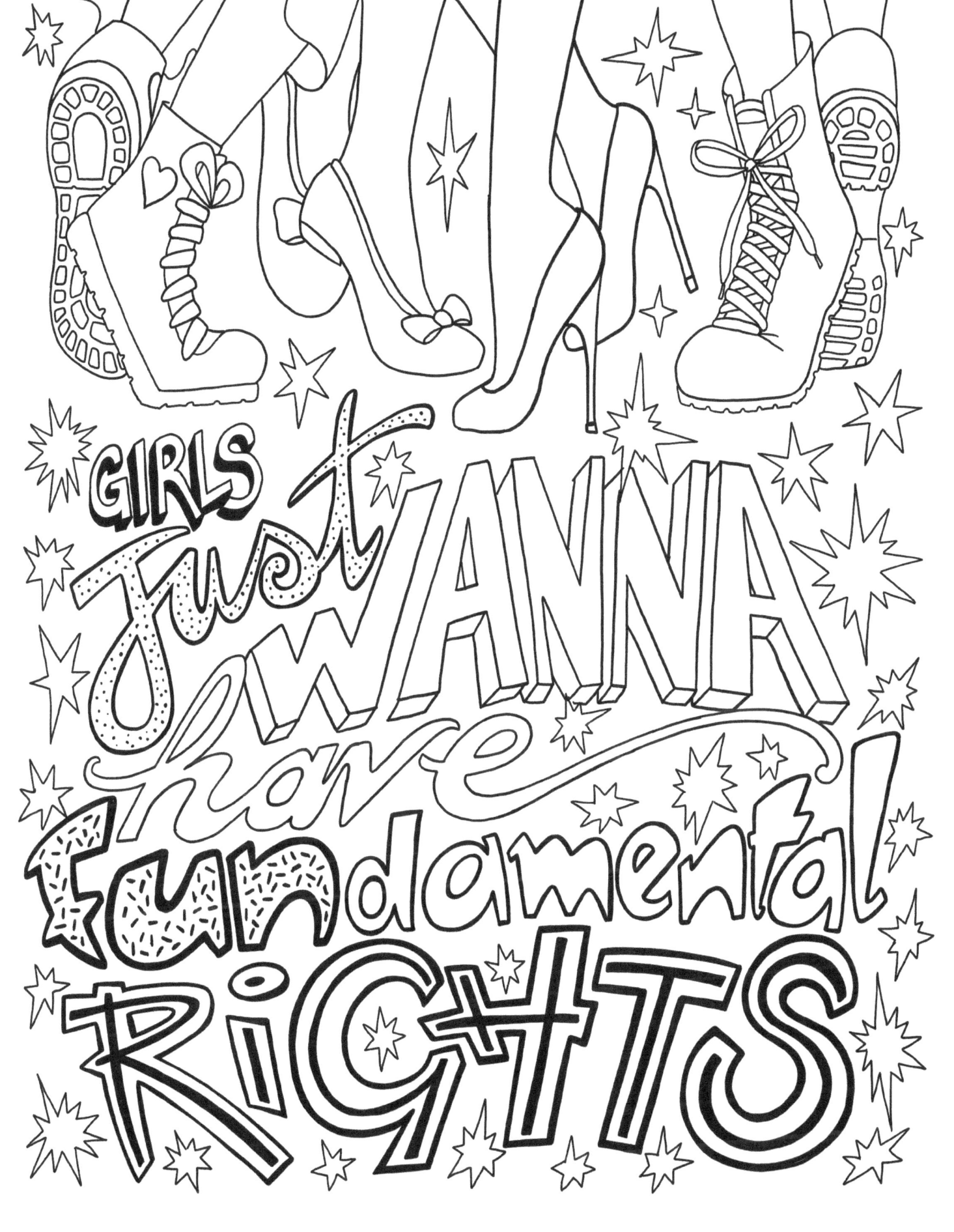

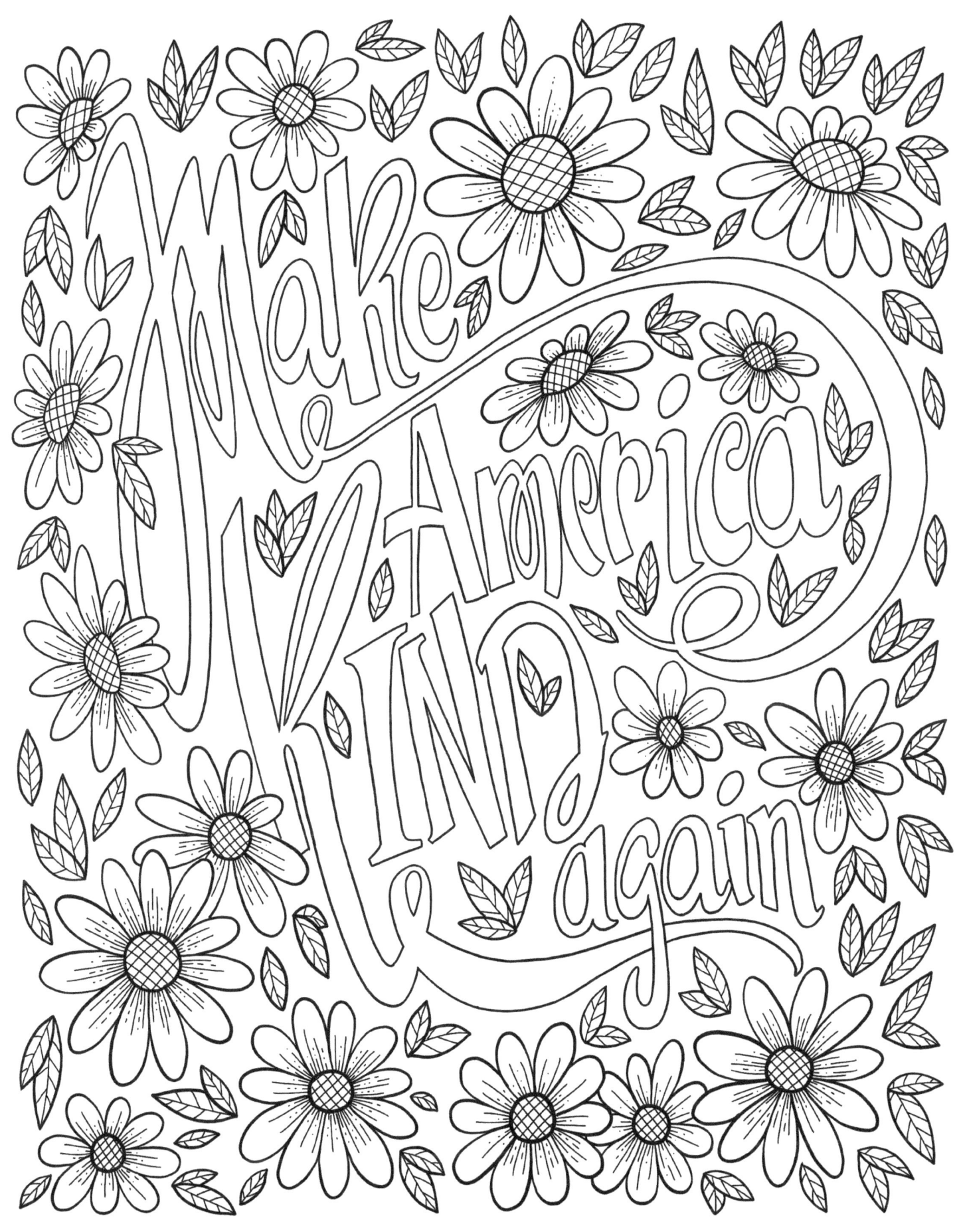

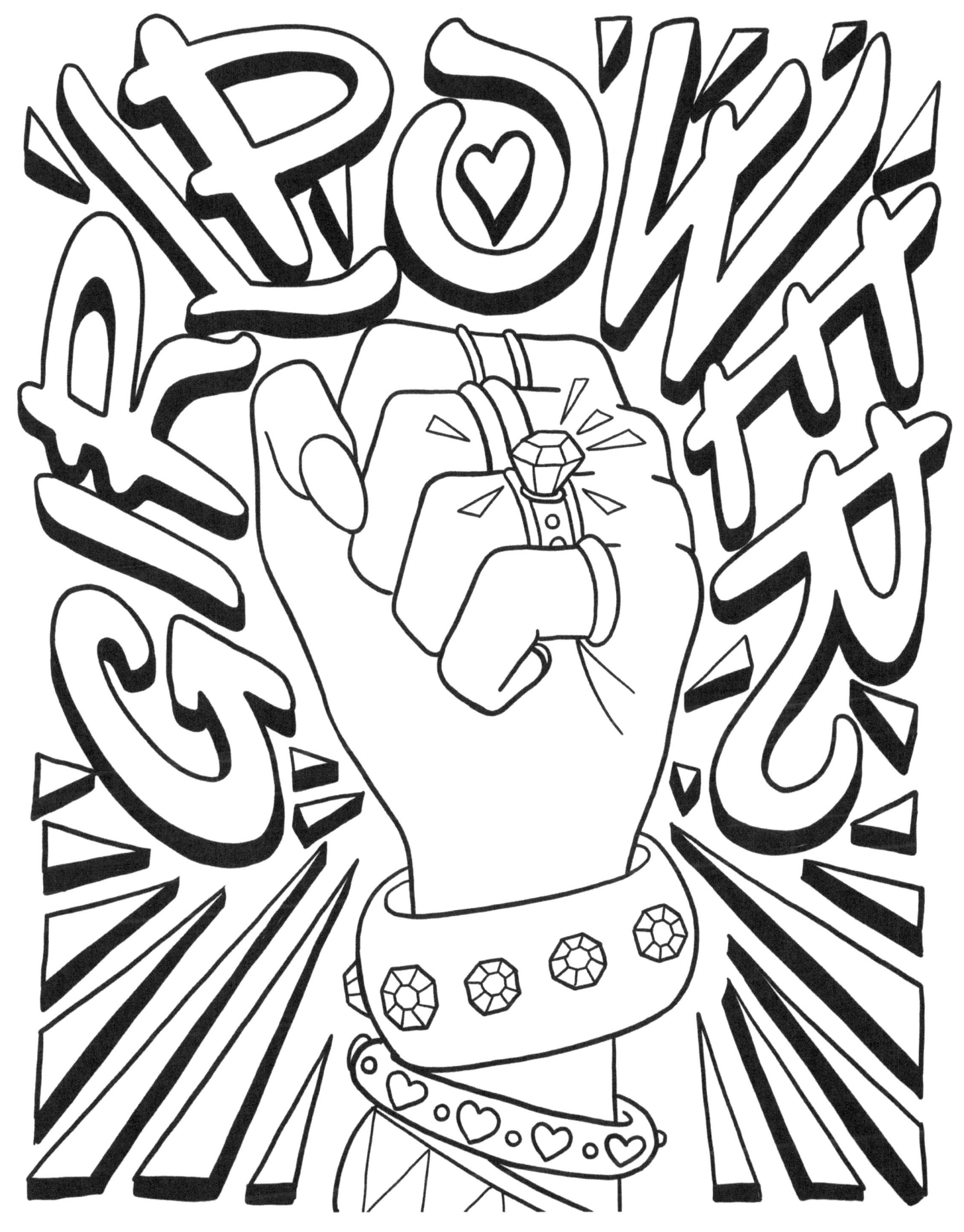

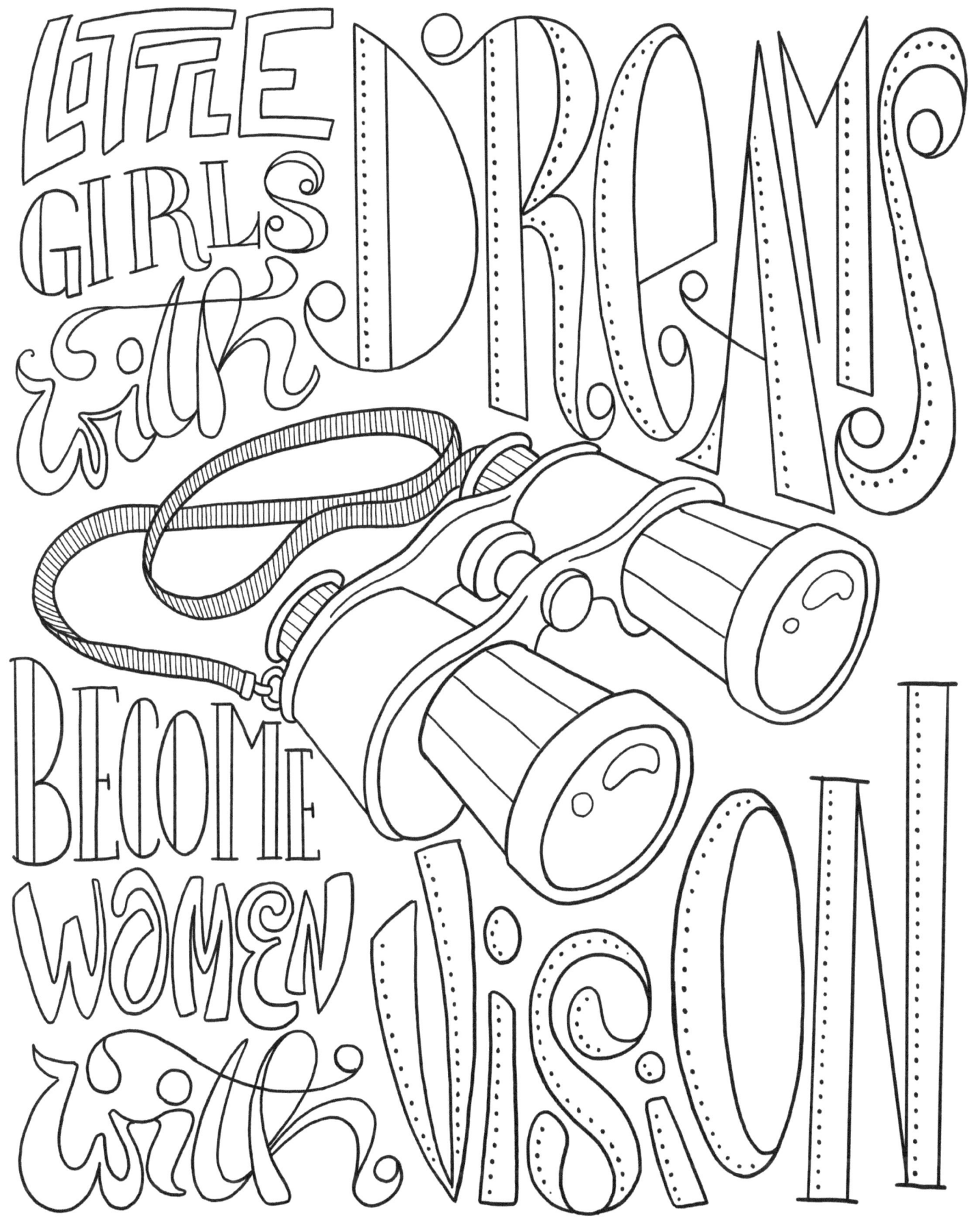

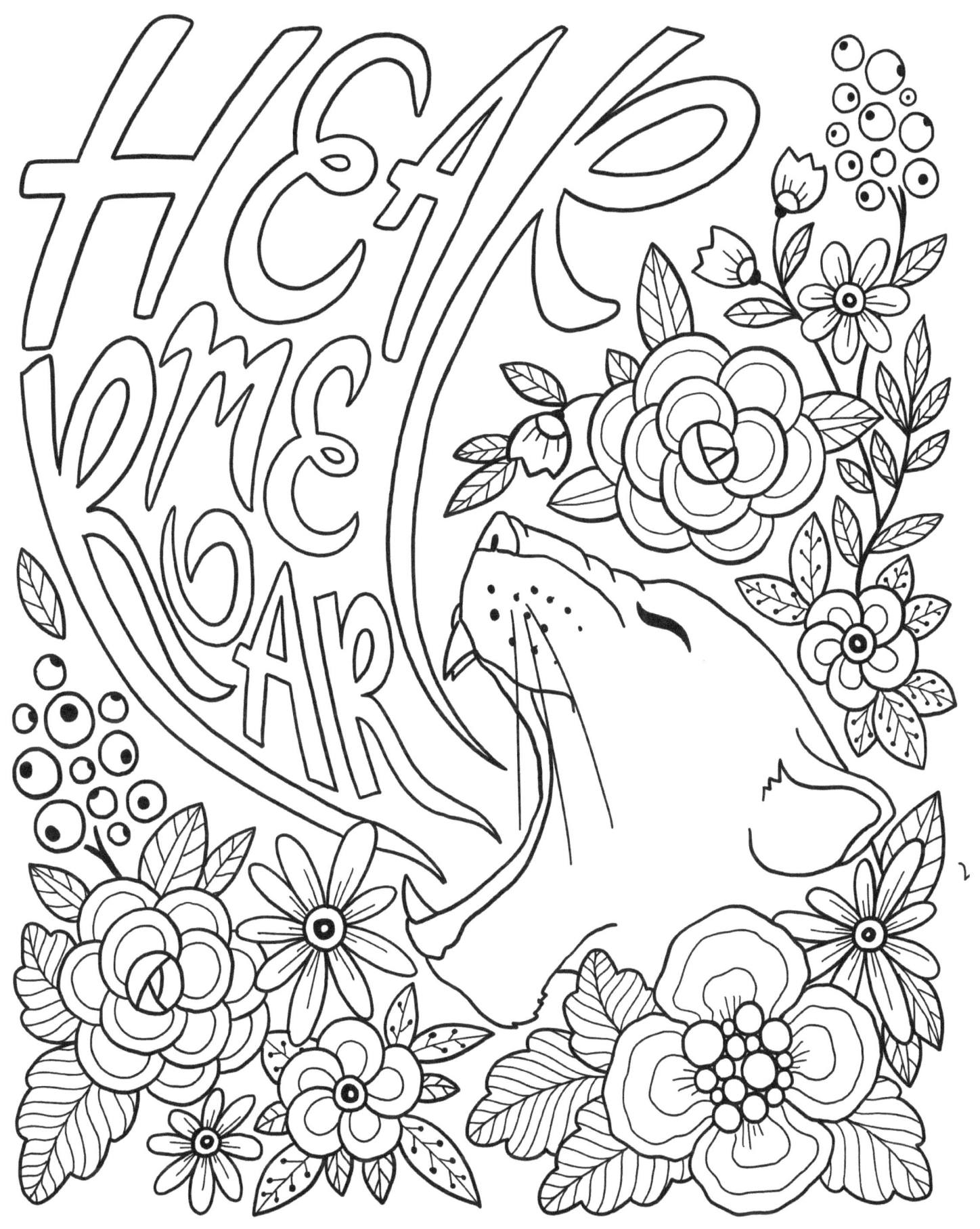

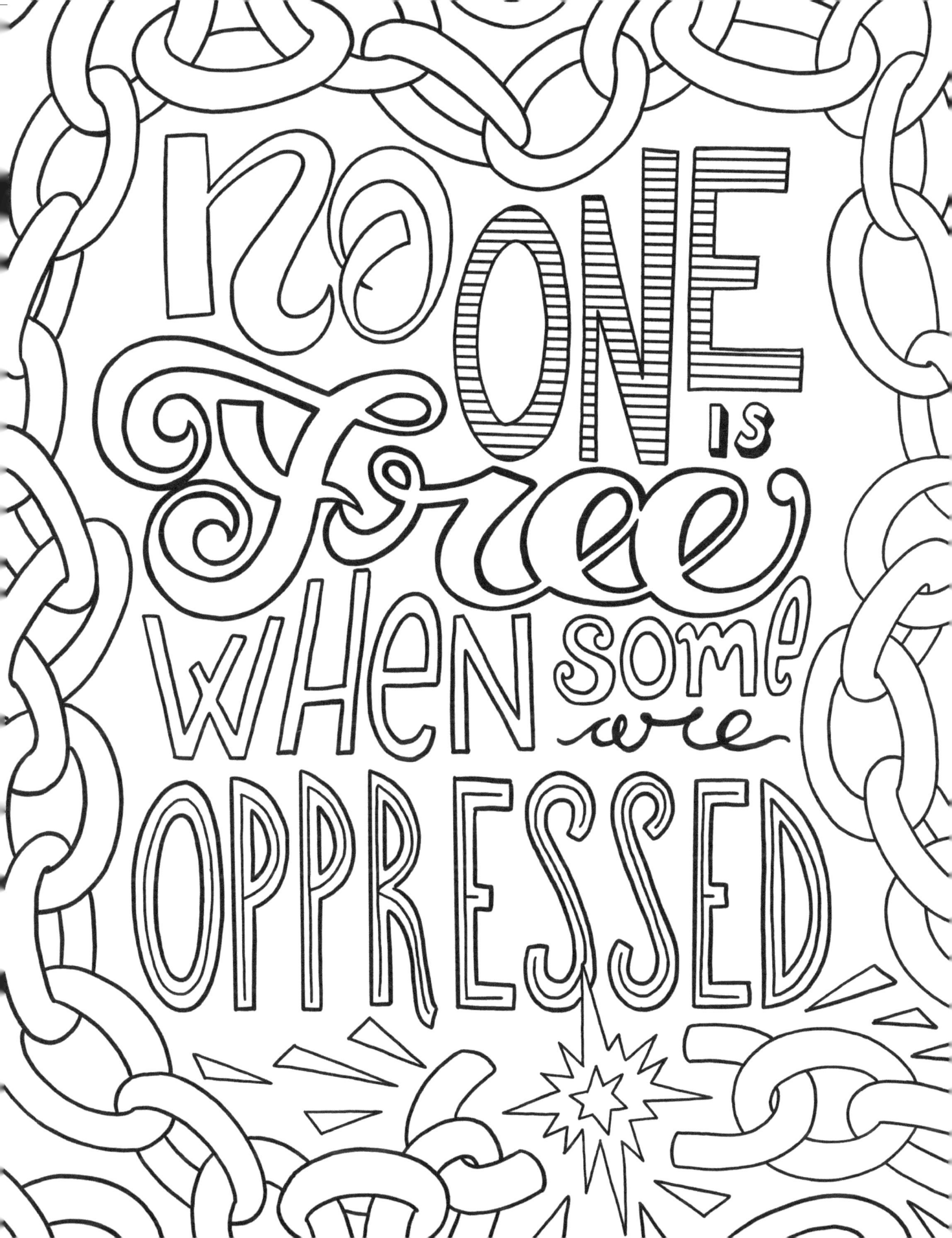

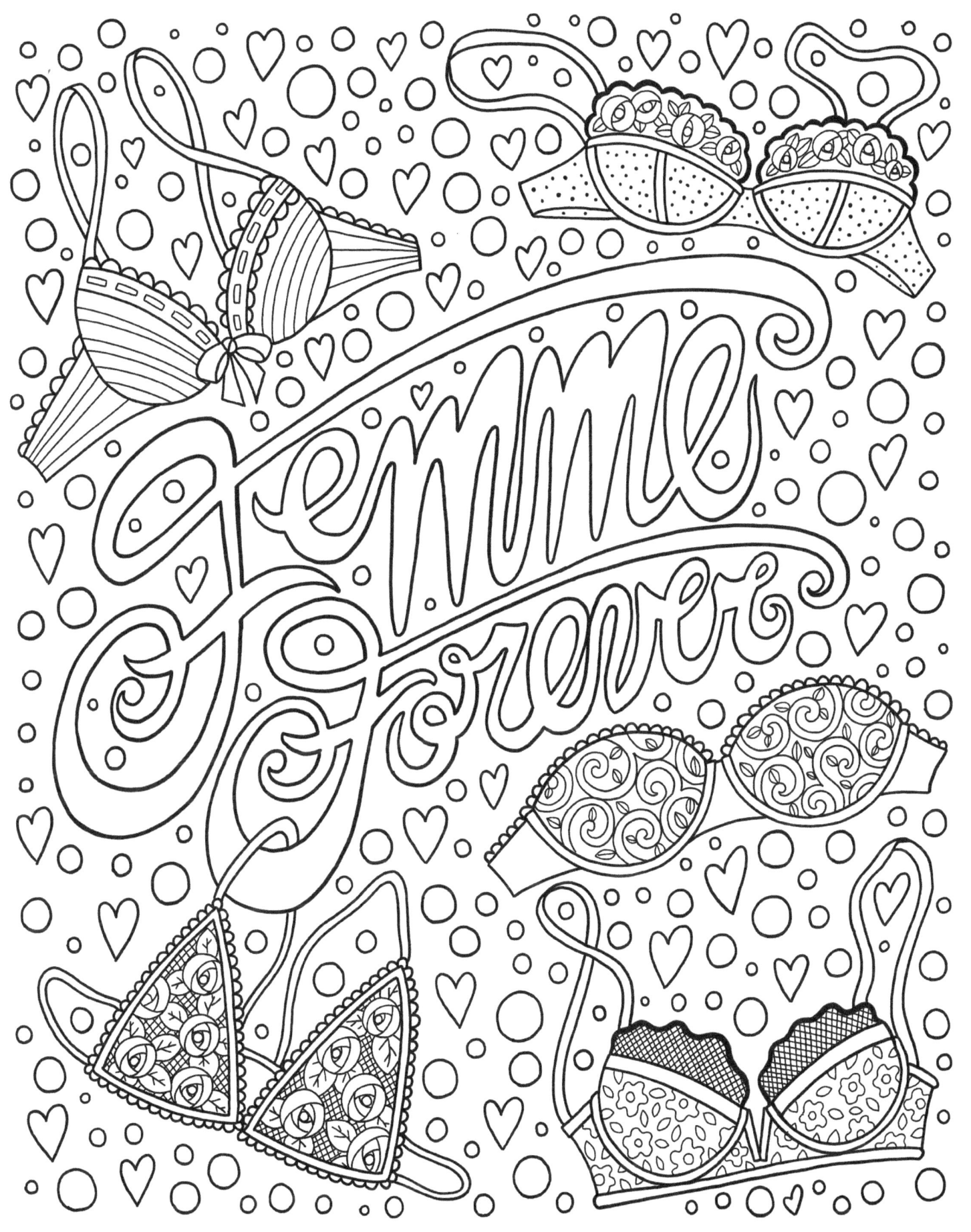

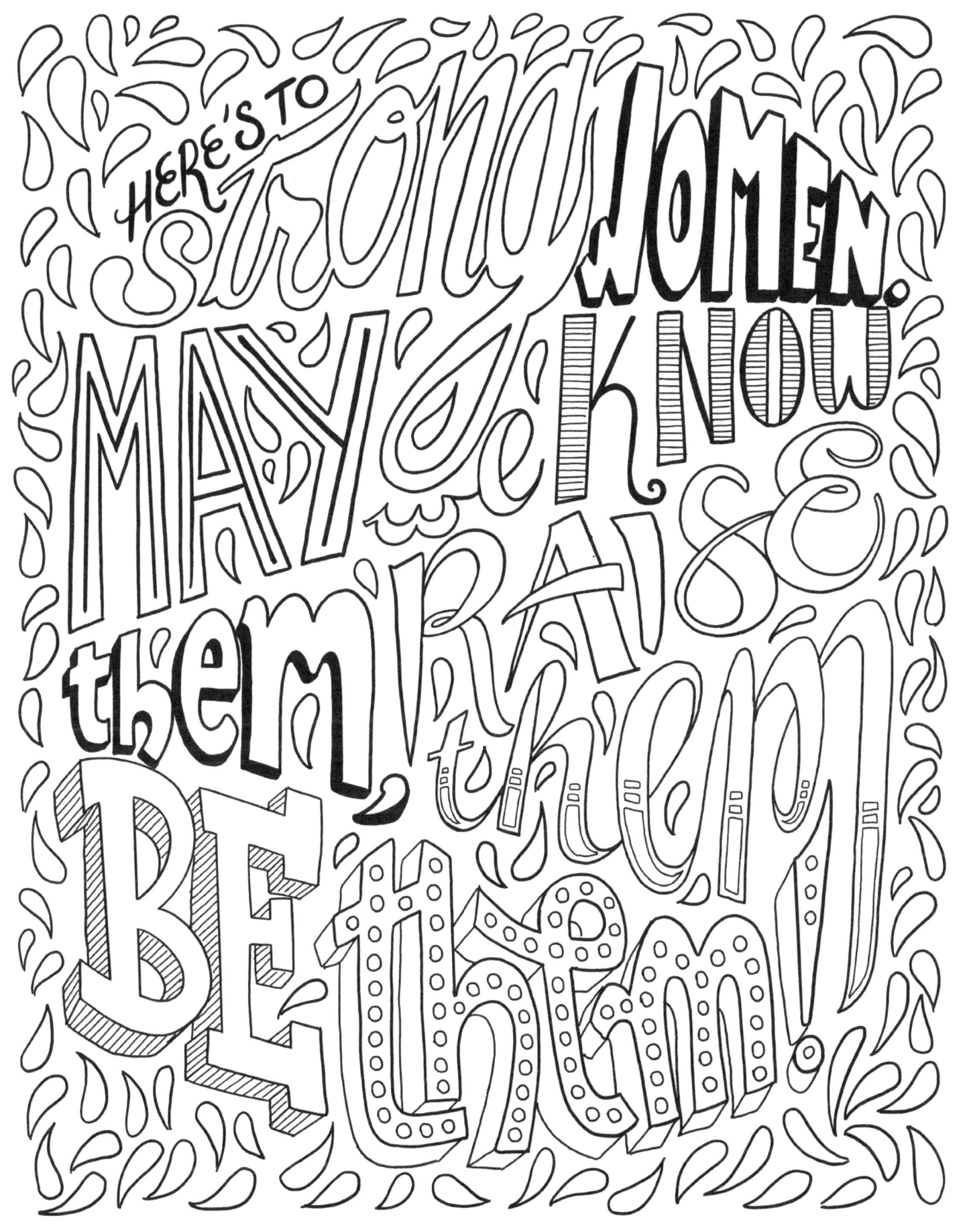

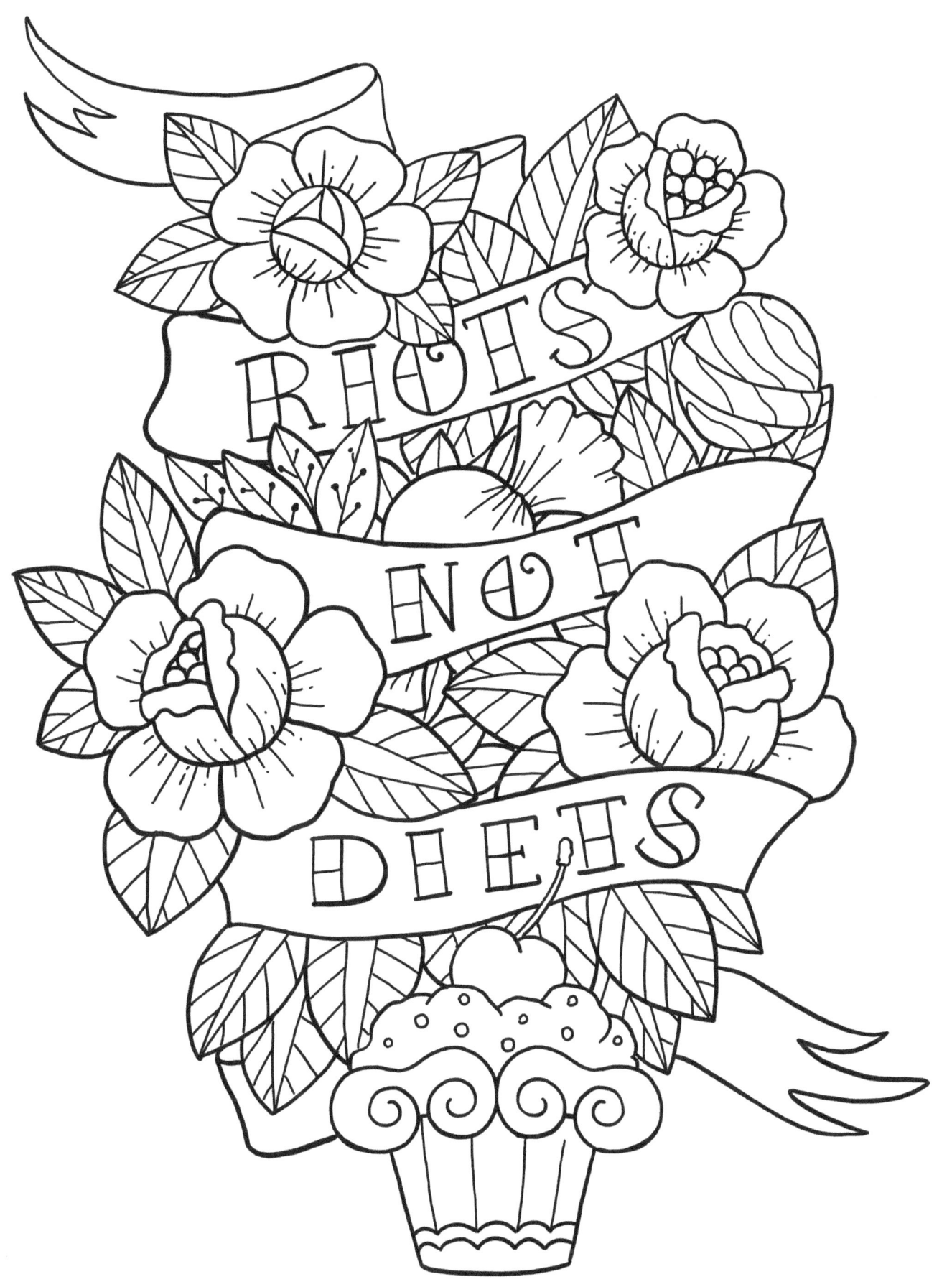

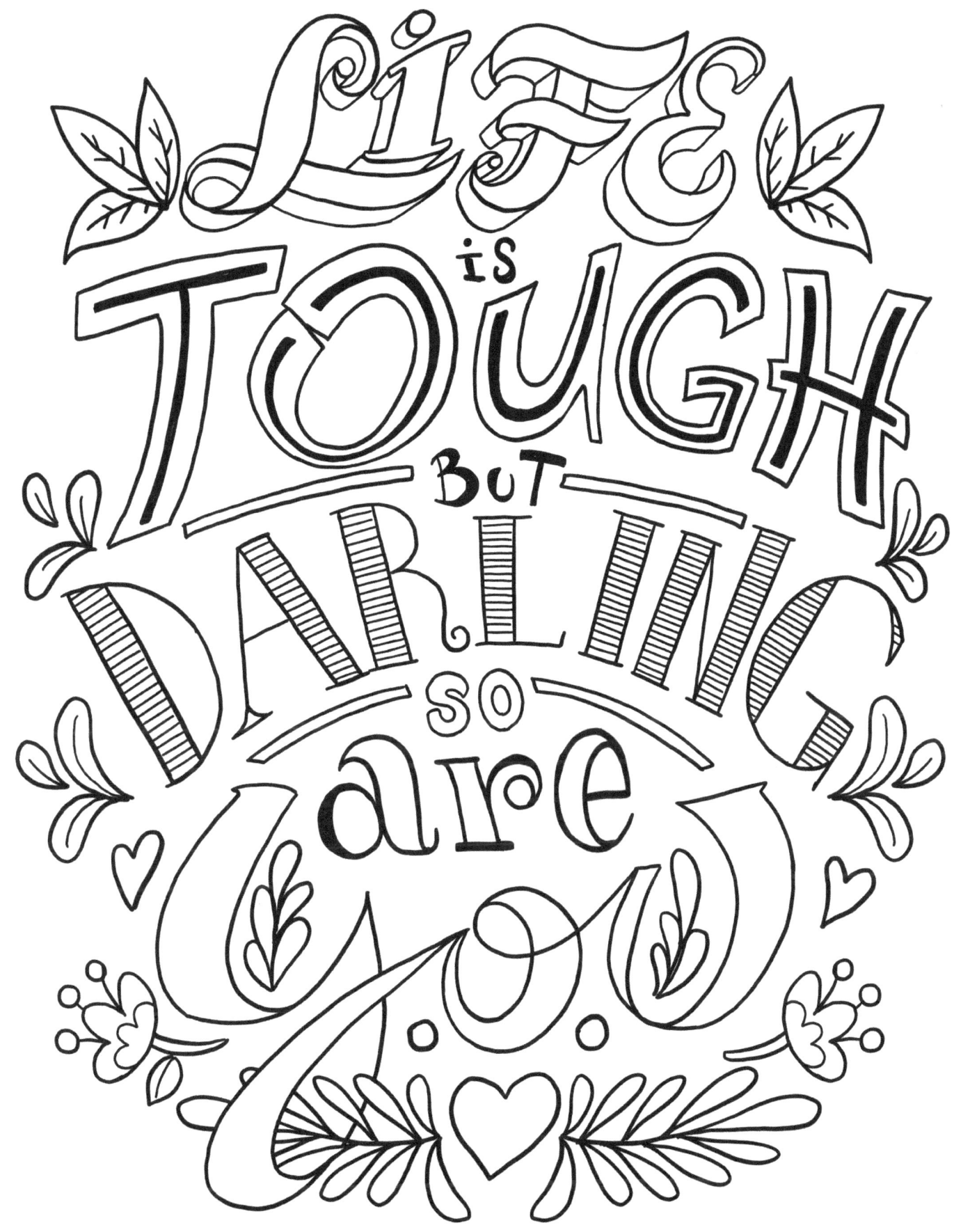

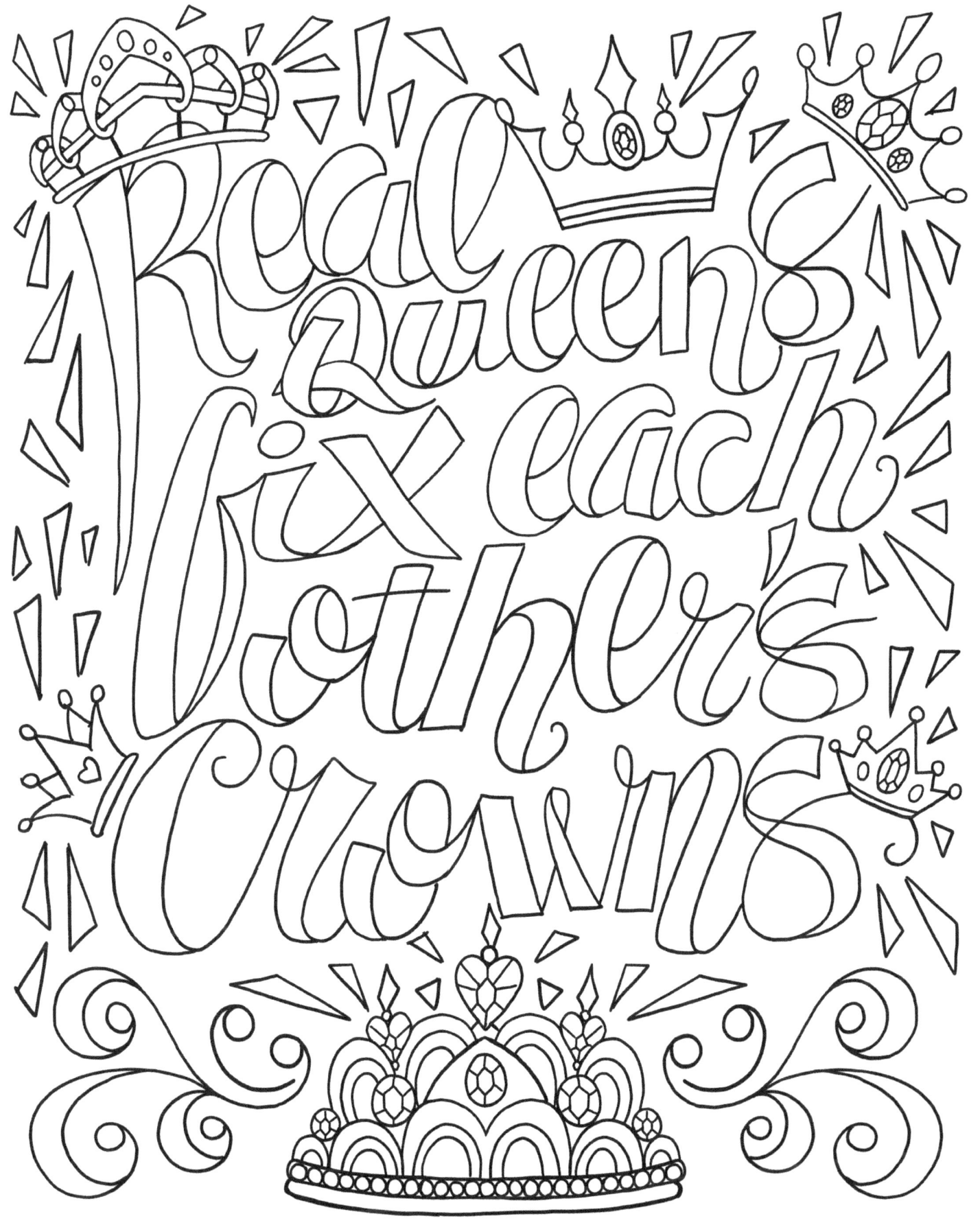

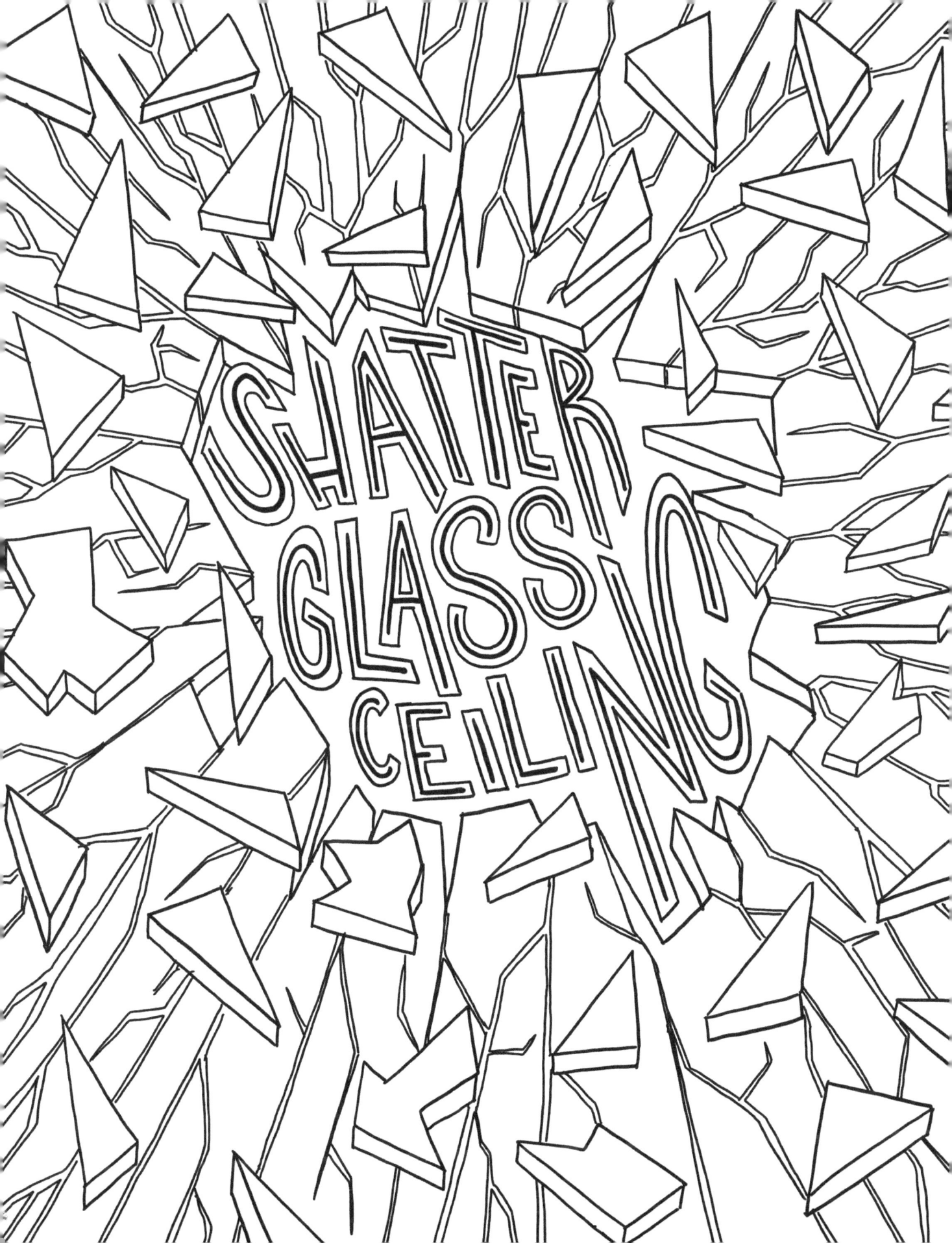

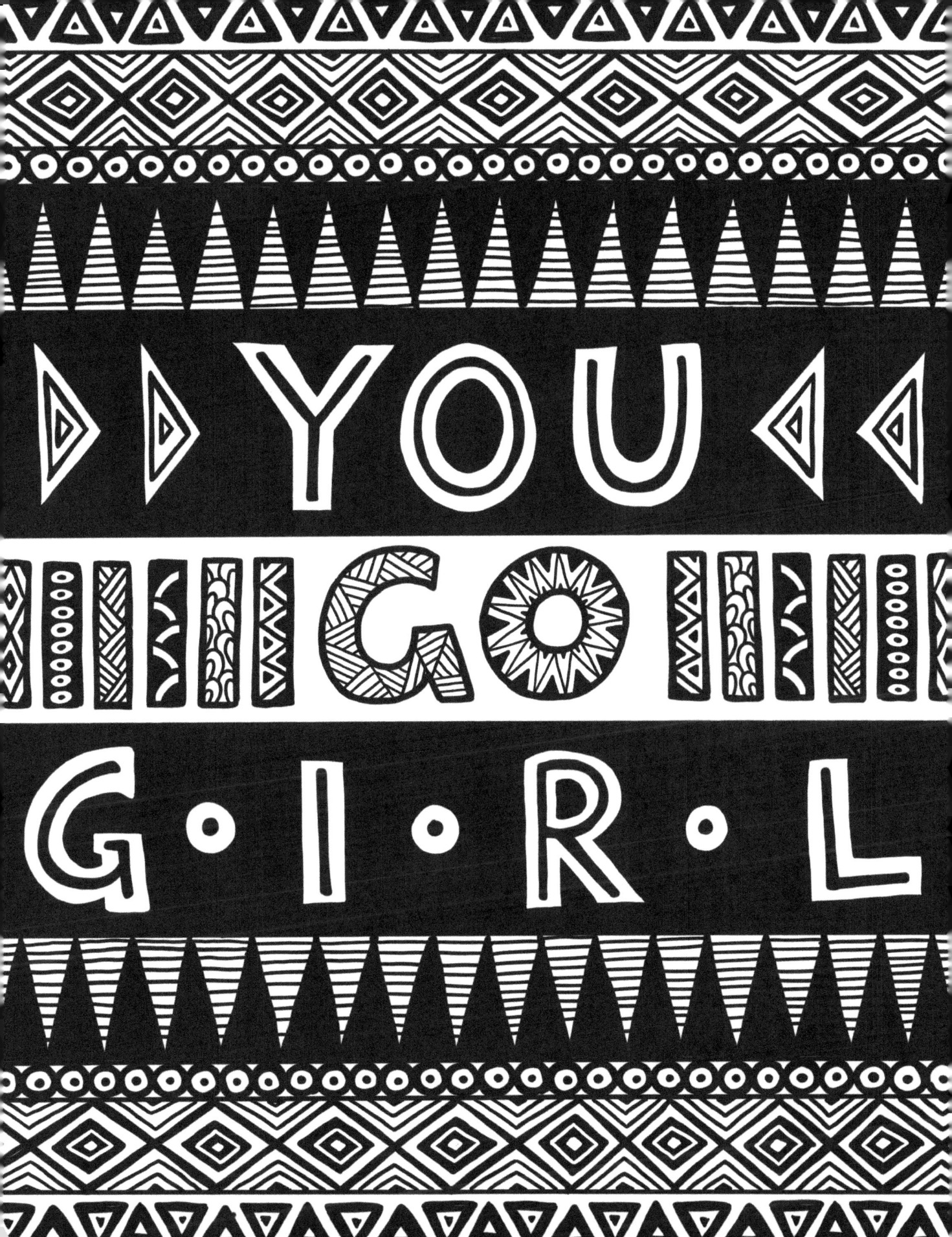

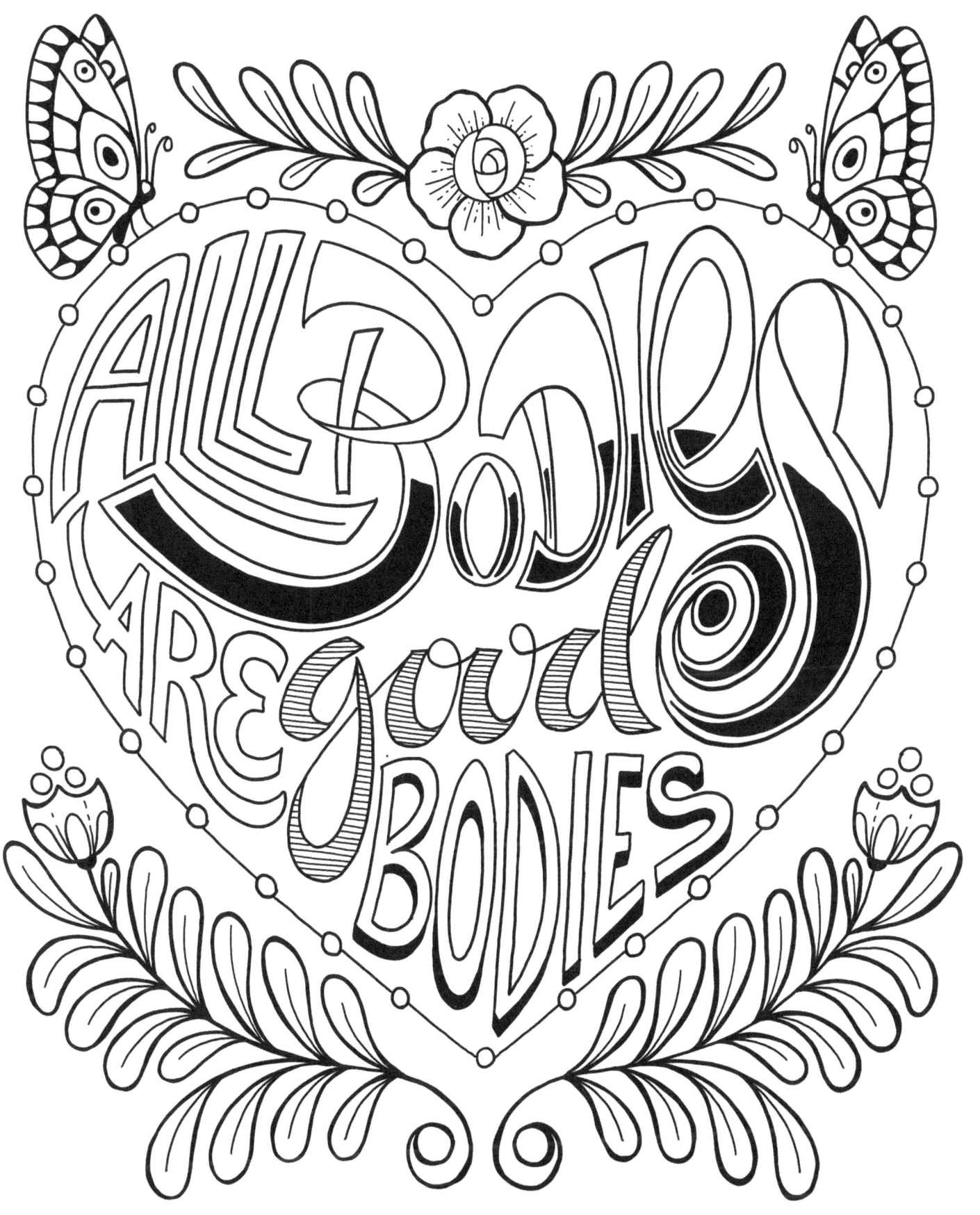

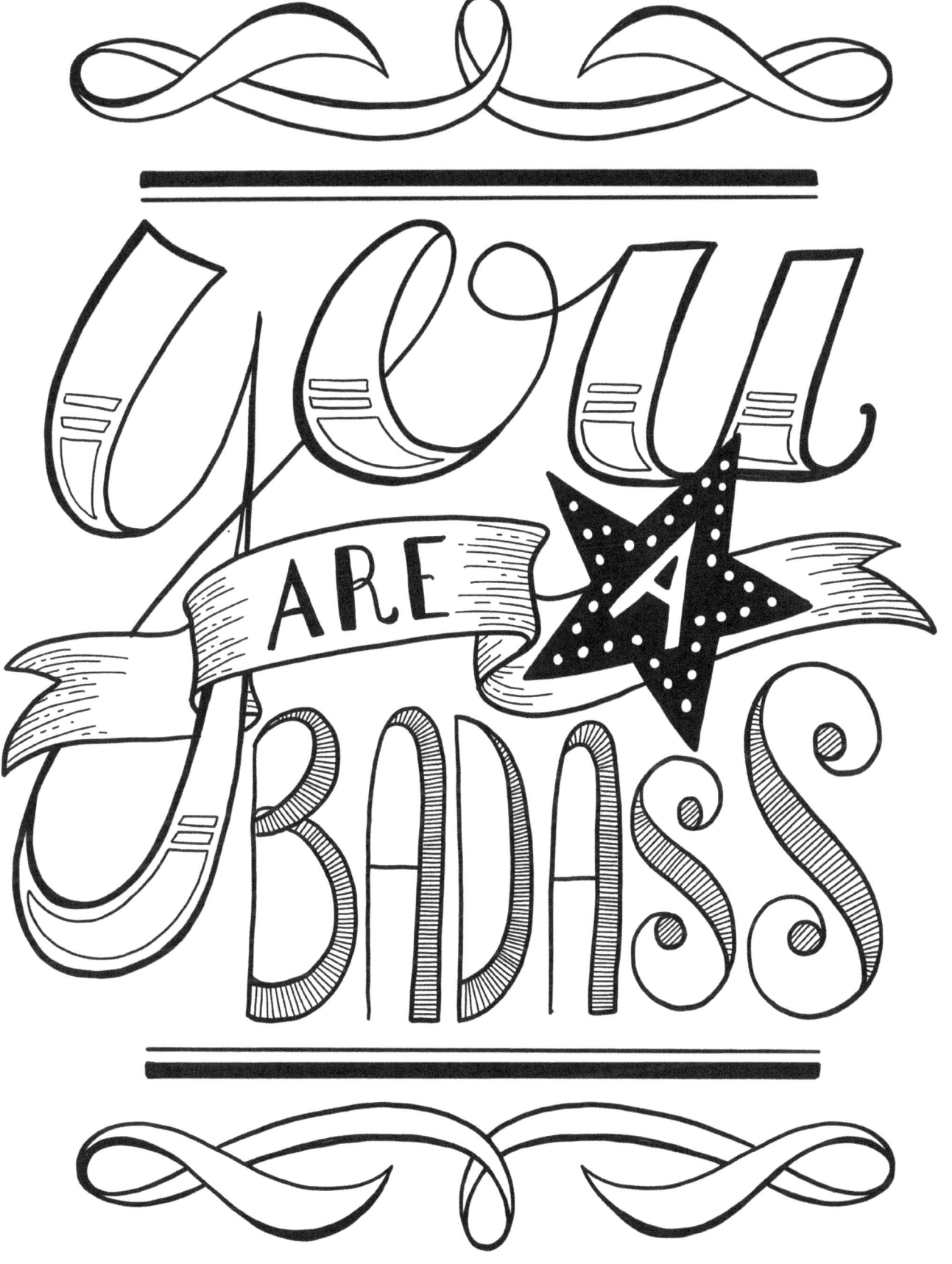

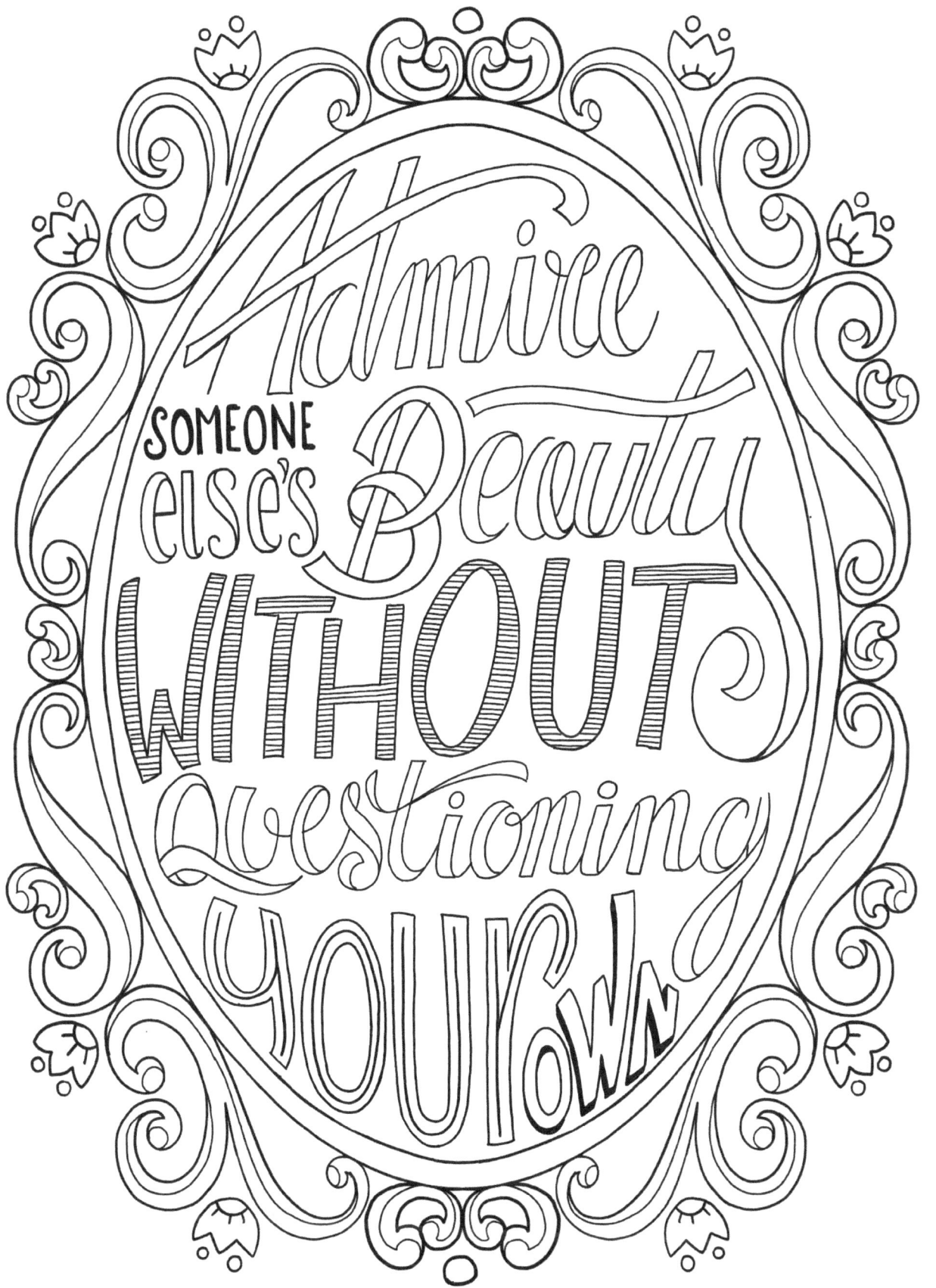

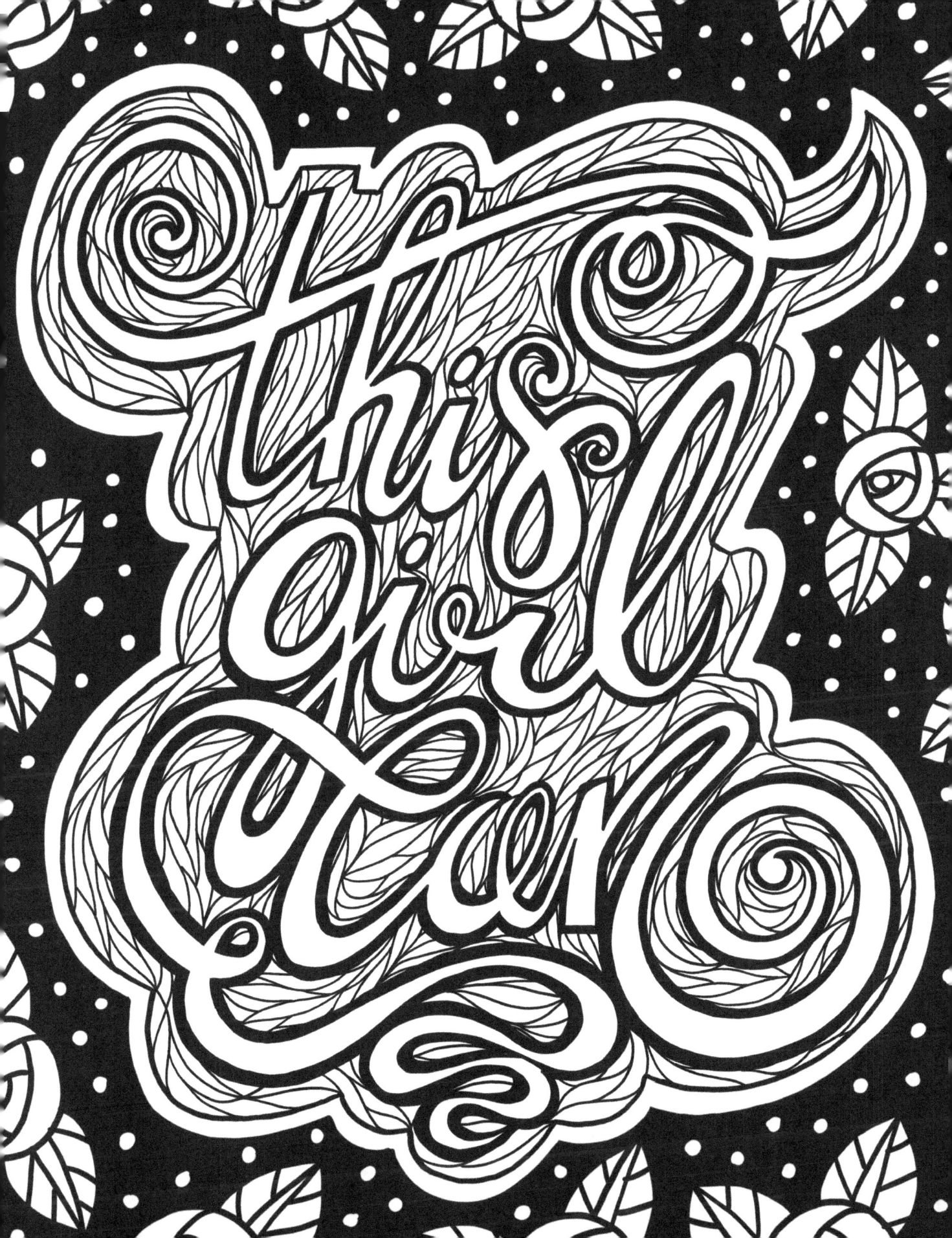

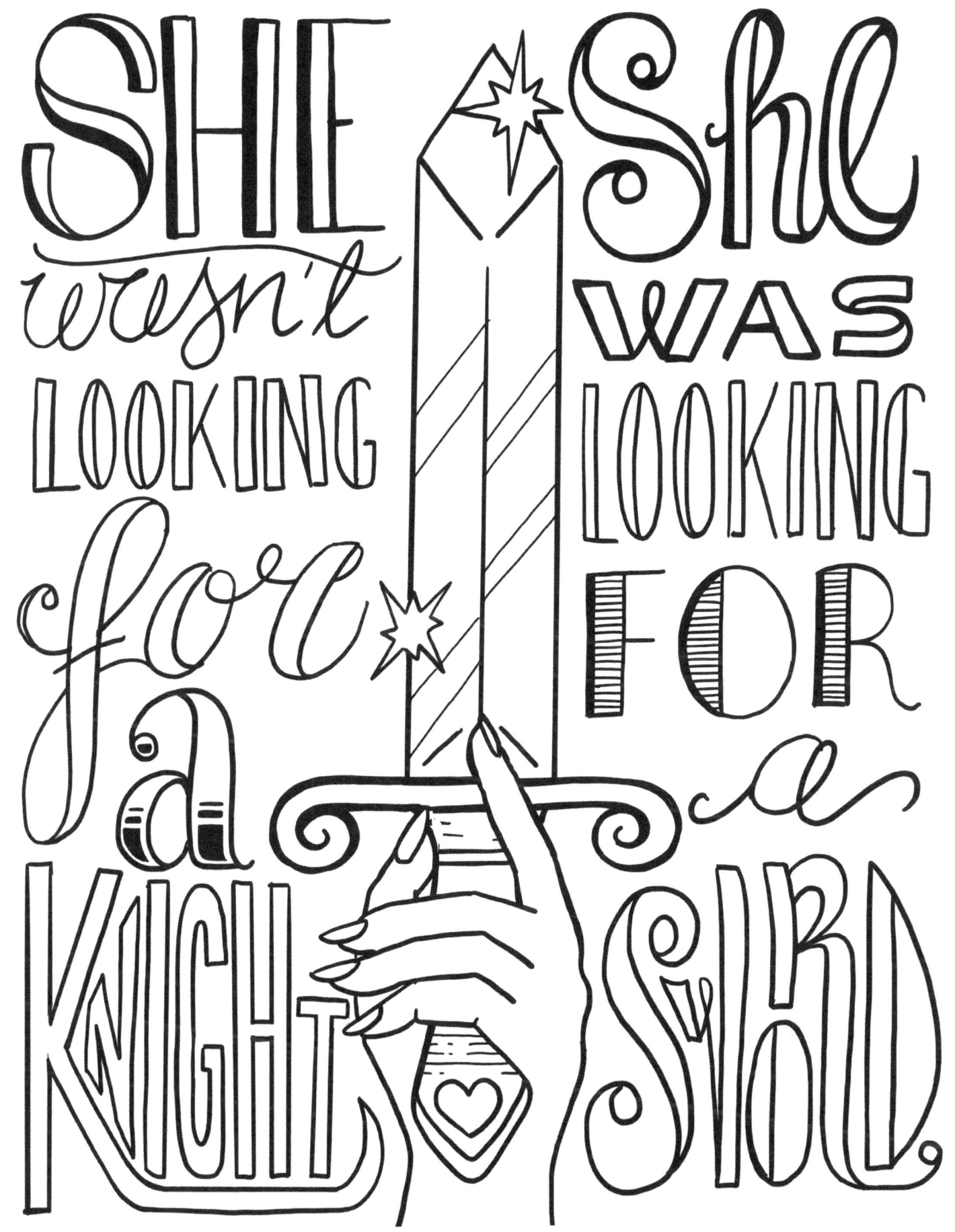

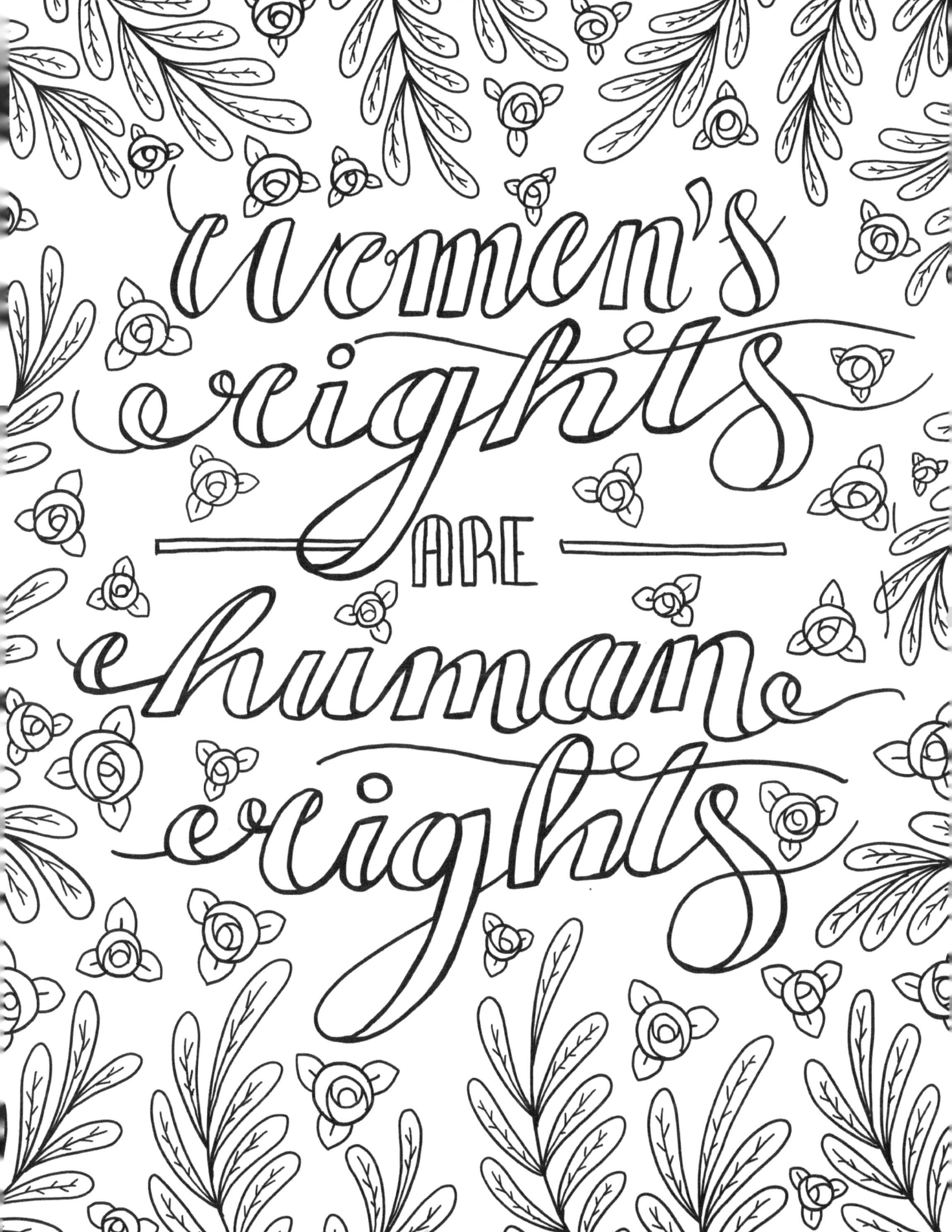

www.ingramcontent.com/pod-product-compliance
Lightning Source LLC
Chambersburg PA
CBHW080836170526
45158CB00009B/2574